Introdi

What is A Gli~~..~~

This book will seek to provide a concise view of the subject and must therefore necessarily leave out much of the detail that can be truly fascinating. A few key events or people will be more closely examined to offer a fuller understanding of some of the issues. Should you wish to delve deeper into the subject there is a suggested further reading list at the end of this book.

I am not a professional historian. I am a passionate amateur, but I have always believed that the key to understanding any historical event, period or topic is understanding the people, not least understanding that they were people. Just like you and I they had hopes, dreams, desires, disasters and disappointments that all came together to make the person remembered to history often as a caricature.

This is not a weighty tome; it is an overview of the subject offering some key details and information. I do not frequently reference source material to avoid making the matter thicker than this view is designed to be.

I hope that you will enjoy reading this book as much as I have enjoyed writing it.

1

Why This Book?

The Wars of the Roses is a fascinating portion of English history. It changed a great deal about England at the time, bringing about the end of the rule of the Plantagenets, still the longest reigning dynasty in British or English history. It paved the way for one of the most famous, and infamous, dynasties in the world, the Tudors. Without the Wars of the Roses, we would never have had cause to hear much about the line descended from a Welsh servant that itself radically altered England forever.

The Wars lasted for most of the second half of the fifteenth century, with occasional outbreaks of peace. The period is named for the White Rose of York and the Red Rose of Lancaster that disputed the right to the English throne, but there is far more to the story than that. There are around one hundred and fifty species of rose at present, and easily as many disputes, small and large, that contributed to the Wars of the Roses.

With a cast including four kings, characters such as Warwick the Kingmaker, Lady Margaret Beaufort and Thomas, Lord Stanley and with the crown passing back and forth it is a fascinating tale of murder, betrayal, intrigue, love and death. There are unknown fates, reputations that live on today and one of the most contentious kings and alleged crimes in English history.

Contents

The Third Period

The Fourth Period

The Fifth Period

The Root of the Roses

When considering how, where or why the Wars of the Roses originated, the blame must be laid in large part at the feet of King Edward III. Edward was King of England for fifty years and is considered to have been, by almost any measure, one of the most successful mediaeval monarchs. Under threat from Edward and his mother, Isabella of France, his father, Edward II abdicated in favour of his son. Edward's rule was long and bathed in glory with military success in France, progressive legislation, the continued development of Parliament and the establishment of the Order of the Garter. In his later years though it is possible that Edward suffered one or more strokes and fell into a period of inactivity that led to military failures by his sons and a surge of abuse of the power he was forced to spread out. His rule had not been without severe problems too; Edward's reign had seen the country and its people ravaged by the Black Death.

Edward and his wife Philippa of Hainault were blessed with nine children who survived childhood, five sons and four daughters. Edward had worked hard to find good marriages for all of his children amongst the royalty of Europe in his efforts to expand his dynasty's influence, yet this brought with it the problems of ambitious children keen for the main prize.

The eldest son and heir to Edward III was Edward, the Black Prince. He was a famed military leader, defeating the French at Crecy and Poitiers and appeared set to reign in his father's mould. He had also developed a reputation for harsh cruelty, often ignoring accepted notions of chivalry both on the battlefield and off it. For example, he employed flank attacks to defeat enemies and often sacked and burned towns to disrupt France.

Edward III's other sons were Lionel of Antwerp, Duke of Clarence who died in 1368 aged 29, John of Gaunt, Duke of Lancaster, Edmund of Langley, Duke of York and Thomas of Woodstock, Duke of Gloucester. It is from John that the House of Lancaster traced its claim and from Edmund that the House of York descended.

On 8th June 1376, at the age of 45, Edward the Black Prince died at Westminster, leaving his nine year old son Richard as the heir to his grandfather's throne. On 21st June the following year, 1377, Edward III died also, making his grandson King Richard II at the age of ten. Due to fears that John of Gaunt would usurp the throne he was excluded from the Council that ruled in the young king's name, though in reality retained a great deal of influence. Richard's minority was long and marked primarily by the Peasants' Revolt, during which Richard reached agreement with the rebels only to go back on his word. Towards the end of the 1390's Richard slipped into a period of tyranny, executing many nobles including his uncle

Thomas. A dispute arose between John of Gaunt's son Henry Bolingbroke and Thomas de Mowbray, Duke of Norfolk. Richard banished both men. Henry returned to England, landing at Ravenspur in Yorkshire in June 1399. Initially claiming he wanted only to regain the Lancastrian lands and titles of the recently deceased John of Gaunt, Henry eventually claimed the throne and Richard was overthrown. Richard's final fate is unclear but it is possible he starved to death in captivity.

Henry Bolingbroke ruled as King Henry IV, the first Lancastrian king. His son Henry V has passed into legend following Agincourt and the conquests made in France. In 1422, Henry V died on campaign, leaving a nine month old son to take the throne as King Henry VI. Henry's minority was longer still than Richard II's. His uncle Humphrey, Duke of Gloucester acted as Protector in England while another uncle John, Duke of Bedford became regent of the French territories. When Henry came of age he favoured seeking a peaceful settlement with France, supported by Cardinal Beaufort, a half-uncle of Henry V and William de la Pole, Earl of Suffolk. This approach was vehemently opposed by the king's uncle Humphrey and by Richard, Duke of York but they were ignored.

As part of the agreement for his marriage to Margaret of Anjou in 1445, Henry agreed to give up land in Maine and Anjou, a move deeply unpopular, particularly with Humphrey and the Duke of York, and which seemed to focus anger upon the Earl of Suffolk who Henry was keen to protect. Lines were drawn at the court of King Henry VI and it is at this point that tensions reached breaking point.

The Great Families

During the mediaeval period England was ruled by a monarch who sat at the summit of the social order. Directly below were the nobility, ranked by title, Duke being the senior followed by Earl, Marquis, Viscount and the emerging gentry titled Lord. The general populace owed allegiance to their Lord, usually the noble who owned the land on which they lived. When called upon to do so, they were required to give service to their lord on the battlefield. They would have possessed little choice in the matter; it was not a question of whether they agreed with their Lord's cause, merely a question of keeping a roof over their family's heads.

The clergy operated alongside this system. They owed their ultimate allegiance to the Pope in Rome and the monarch was not normally permitted to interfere in matters of ecclesiastical justice. Bishops and Archbishops often served within the political body as members of the Council and many had a great impact upon the political world. A career in the church could provide a way through life for a younger noble son unlikely to inherit anything of his own or for ambitious men from non-noble backgrounds.

During the Wars of the Roses there were many great noble families in England, members of which played pivotal roles in the swinging of the pendulum of power. Some remained staunchly loyal to one side, others did not. Both courses could bring trouble as one side gained the upper hand, then the other, punishing opponents whilst neither was sure whether some support could be trusted.

It is worth considering the pedigree of the Royal Houses of York and Lancaster, since the quality of the claim each possessed was to prove vital and contentious. It is also hard to describe the family relationships at this time clearly. Many people possessed the same names, titles changed hands as male lines petered out and marriage to a cousin, in some degree or other, was commonplace. John of Gaunt alone presents a complex figure from whom both Lancastrian and Yorkist kings and many senior nobles could claim descent. Issues such as this created complex loyalties, even within families, and would serve to muddy the waters that nourished the Wars of the Roses.

The House of Lancaster

The House that traces its lineage from its founder John of Gaunt, Duke of Lancaster, third son of King Edward III was the richest and one of the most powerful families in England by the end of the fourteenth century. The Duchy of Lancaster continues to this day to provide a major source of income for the crown. John of Gaunt was uncle to King Richard II. Born in 1340, he was created Earl of Richmond as a child and entered the Order of the Garter in 1359 on the death of one of its original members. He was married first to Blanche of Lancaster and on her father's death he acquired the Dukedom of Lancaster along with the Earldoms of Derby, Leicester and Lincoln and became Steward of England. Blanche died in 1369 leaving John with three children, Henry (later King Henry IV), Philippa (who became Queen of Portugal) and Elizabeth (who married John Holland, Duke of Exeter). John's second marriage was to Constance of Castile and produced only one daughter, Catherine, who would become Queen of Castile and is an ancestor of Catherine of Aragon.

When Constance died in 1394, John married his mistress Katherine Swynford in 1396. Their illegitimate children were legitimised in Parliament by Richard II, later confirmed by Henry IV and Henry V, though the act of legitimacy strictly forbade them or their descendants from claiming the throne. The children took the name Beaufort after the castle in France where they were born. These children were John, Earl of Somerset, who was the ancestor through whom Henry VII's mother claimed royal descent, Cardinal Henry Beaufort, Thomas, Duke of Exeter and Joan who married Ralph Neville, Earl of Westmorland. Joan was grandmother to Warwick the Kingmaker, King Edward IV and King Richard III.

John's military career was extensive in France and Spain but never very successful, making him unpopular at home. When Edward III's oldest son, the Black Prince, died leaving a child heir there appears to have been genuine concern that John would seek to take the throne for himself. He was ordered to swear an oath of allegiance to Richard, which he did. With his eldest brother's death, John's influence grew at the court of his aging, ill father. When Edward III died, John was excluded from the minority Council of Richard II though in reality he retained a great deal of power and influence.

King Richard II banished John's son Henry Bolingbroke in 1398 following a dispute. When John died in early 1399, Henry was not permitted to attend the funeral and returned to England a few months later claiming that he wished only to be reconciled with the king and to claim his inheritance of the Duchy of Lancaster. Landing at Ravenspur in Yorkshire, he headed south gathering support and momentum. When he arrived in London, he was strong enough to swiftly depose the unpopular

Richard and install himself as King Henry IV. Richard was kept in captivity but a later attempt to free him made his continued existence untenable. Reports claim that he was starved to death, though others stated that he starved himself to death, and probably died on 14th February 1400, aged 33.

This event was vital because it severed the line of succession and challenged the notion that kings were appointed by God. A man had dared to remove a king and a dangerous precedent was set by the House of Lancaster which was to haunt it for decades to come. As king, Henry IV suffered many rebellions. In Wales, Owain Glyndwr was fighting for independence and in England the Percy family, led by the Earl of Northumberland, rebelled. Henry managed to crush these uprisings but never felt secure on his throne. Following several periods of illness, Henry died on 20th March 1413 aged 46. Henry's first wife Mary de Bohun had provided him with four sons and two daughters and it was the eldest son who became King Henry V aged about 27. Henry V's exploits in France are legendary. He succeeded in regaining much of Edward III's French lands and was immensely popular at home as a result. His victory at Agincourt saw him immortalised. Yet Henry died in 1422, in his mid thirties, probably from dysentery. His only child was a nine month old boy also named Henry. It was this king of the House of Lancaster who sat upon the throne as building tensions exploded and politics spiralled out of control into the open warfare we now call the Wars of the Roses.

The House of York

The founder of the House of York was Edmund of Langley, 1st Duke of York. Edmund was born on 5th June 1341, the fourth surviving son of King Edward III. In 1361 he was made a Knight of the Garter and in 1362, aged 21, became Earl of Cambridge. He undertook several campaigns in France for his father and though he was not outstanding, neither was he a military failure.

Edmund was married firstly to Isabella, daughter of King Peter of Castile. They had three children; Edward of Norwich, 2nd Duke of York who was killed fighting alongside Henry V at Agincourt, Richard of Conisburgh, Earl of Cambridge, who was executed for treason by Henry V but who is an ancestor of King Edward IV and King Richard III, and Constance of York, an ancestor of Anne Neville, wife of King Richard III.

Richard of Conisburgh was executed on 5th August 1415 and Edward, Duke of York was killed at the Battle of Agincourt on 25th October the same year. On Edward's death without children, the title Duke of York passed to his nephew, Richard, son of the executed Richard of Conisburgh who was not yet quite 4 years of age. This Richard became 3rd Duke of York and was a prime mover in the Wars of the Roses. Usually referred to as Richard of York, he was the father of King Edward IV and King Richard III.

As a child with an enormous inheritance, Richard's wardship was valuable and was granted to Ralph Neville, Earl of Westmorland, who had over twenty children by his two wives and needed good matches for his many daughters. Ralph, as he was entitled to do with his ward, married Richard to his daughter Cecily when Richard was 13 and Cecily 9. Cecily was called the Rose of Raby for her beauty and the couple appear to have enjoyed a happy marriage, at least until the eruption of the Wars of the Roses. Richard of York had a distinguished military career in France before being made Lieutenant of Ireland and Earl of Ulster. Irish support, based upon this connection, was to prove a great boon to the House of York in times of trouble.

At the emergence of trouble in the mid 1450's, Richard Duke of York was the senior noble in the country and one of the richest and most powerful men in the land.

House Beaufort

The Beaufort family were the illegitimate children of John of Gaunt and his long time mistress Katherine Swynford. Eventually the children were declared legitimate and John and Katherine married, though the Beauforts and all of their descendants were specifically barred from succession to the throne of England. This may have reflected the ambitious threat John was perceived to be to the childless Richard II.

The eldest son, John Beaufort, was created Earl of Somerset while the second, Henry Beaufort, joined the clergy, finally being appointed as Bishop of Winchester, created Cardinal Beaufort and serving as Chancellor several times under his half-brother Henry IV and nephew Henry V. Thomas Beaufort was made Duke of Exeter, serving both Henry IV and Henry V before dying without children. The only daughter, Joan Beaufort, married her second husband Ralph Neville, Earl of Westmorland and her children included Cecily Neville, who married Richard Duke of York.

Joan Beaufort's line was to prove significant but it is the descendants of the eldest son, John Beaufort, Earl of Somerset who were to prove instrumental in the Wars of the Roses. John married Margaret Holland, daughter of the Earl of Kent and they had six children. The eldest was Henry who succeeded to his father's earldom but died without children at the

Siege of Rouen in 1418. The second son was John Beaufort who became Earl of Somerset on his brother's death. Created Duke of Somerset by Henry VI in 1443, John proved a poor military commander. Eventually, whilst ill in 1443, John mistakenly led a force against a town in Brittany friendly to England. He returned to England in disgrace and died the following year, with rumour growing that he had taken his own life. John had only one child, a daughter, Margaret Beaufort, who became the richest heiress in England and whose impact would be felt keenly some forty years after her father's death.

John's other siblings included Joan Beaufort who married King James I of Scotland and Edmund Beaufort, who succeeded John as 2nd Duke of Somerset and was to come into conflict with Richard of York. This duke had many children; his sons Henry the 3rd Duke of Somerset, Edmund the 4th Duke and John, Earl of Dorset were to become key Lancastrian leaders during the ensuing civil strife.

Margaret Beaufort, daughter of John, 1st Duke of Somerset was placed in the care of the half-brothers of King Henry VI, Edmund and Jasper Tudor. She was married to Edmund Tudor, by who she had her only child, Henry Tudor, later King Henry VII. Margaret was 12 when she married the 24 year old Edmund and she gave birth the following year aged 13. Edmund died before Henry was born and Margaret later married Sir Henry Stafford, son of the Duke of Buckingham and then Thomas, Lord Stanley, later Earl of Derby.

Margaret devoted her life to her only son and her drive served to create the Tudor dynasty.

House Neville

The Neville family were an immensely powerful northern affinity. Alongside, and often in opposition to, the Percy family Earls of Northumberland, the Nevilles oversaw the north of England, far away from the Court in London. Ralph Neville was created Earl of Westmorland by King Richard II in reward for his support against the Lord Appellant in 1397. Ralph Neville first married Margaret Stafford with whom he had eight children. When she died he married Joan Beaufort, daughter of John of Gaunt. Ralph's loyalties were therefore tested when his king took against his new family. When Henry Bolingbroke landed, Ralph supported him and was in the deputation at the Tower of London that received the abdication of King Richard II.

By his death in 1425, Ralph had a further fourteen children with his second wife, some of who would become significant political figures and would take a substantial role in the Wars of the Roses. His eldest son with Joan was Richard Neville who, via his mother, became 5th Earl of Salisbury. Richard was the father of the Earl of Warwick who was to become known to history as the Kingmaker. Richard's youngest sister, Cecily, married Richard of York, joining the royal family and making the two Richards brothers-in-law. Robert Neville served as Bishop of Salisbury, William Neville, another son, became Earl of Kent after switching allegiance from Lancaster to York. Several of Ralph and Joan's other children formed a large part of the minor nobility in the north.

House Stafford

The Earls of Stafford were an established English noble family. When Thomas Stafford, the 3rd Earl of Stafford married Anne of Gloucester in 1390, the family joined with royal blood. Anne was the daughter of Thomas of Woodstock, Duke of Gloucester, youngest son of King Edward III. However, Thomas Stafford died two years later without children.

In 1398, Anne married Thomas's younger brother Edmund, now 5th Earl of Stafford following the death of his other elder brother William, the 4th Earl. Edmund and Anne had a son and two daughters. Their son, Humphrey Stafford, became a military leader of renown during both the Hundred Years War and the Wars of the Roses. When his mother died in 1438, Humphrey acquired half of her inheritance, including the Earldom of Buckingham. In 1444 he was further ennobled as Duke of Buckingham and in 1447 made the senior English duke of non-royal blood.

Humphrey married Anne Neville, daughter of Ralph Neville, Earl of Westmorland, the Earl with the surplus of daughters. By this marriage he became brother-in-law to Richard, Duke of York and to Richard Neville, 5th Earl of Salisbury. The couple had many children, the eldest two sons marrying into the Beaufort family. Humphrey Stafford, the oldest son, married Margaret Beaufort, daughter of Edmund, 2nd Duke of Somerset. Humphrey pre-deceased his father so the

Dukedom passed to their son, Henry. Humphrey's brother, Henry, married Lady Margaret Beaufort, daughter of John, 1st Duke of Somerset.

Henry Stafford, 2nd Duke of Buckingham was to become a significant figure during the latter part of the Wars of the Roses and his descendants were prominent at the Tudor court, not always to their good.

House Stanley

One of the most contentious families of this period was the Stanleys. Thomas, 1st Baron Stanley lived from 1405 to 1459. Continuing his father's work, he had successfully built up substantial land and power in the northwest of England. Having served as Lord Chamberlain of Ireland in the 1430's, Thomas was appointed Comptroller of the Royal Household and in 1455 became Lord Chamberlain. By 1456, he was summoned to the House of Lords as Lord Stanley and was invested as a Knight of the Garter. Lord Stanley also held the title of King of Mann.

Thomas and his wife Joan had three sons and three daughters. The two oldest sons, Thomas and William were to become major figures in the Wars of the Roses developing a very distinct reputation. By the time Thomas succeeded his father the Stanleys had risen in three generations from obscurity to wealth and power. They were a family on the very cusp of real, lasting, significant power when the Wars of the Roses erupted.

House Tudor

The Tudors are often portrayed as erupting from nowhere to take the throne of England. Whilst this is true to some extent, it does not tell the whole of their story. Owen Tudor could claim descent from an ancient Welsh noble family, counting the Welsh prince Rhys ap Gruffudd amongst his ancestors. During Owain Glyndwr's rebellion, Owen's father and uncles were staunch supporters of Glyndwr.

When the rebellion ebbed, the family lost their lands to the English crown and Owen's father Meredith sought to rebuild his fortunes in London. Welsh families rarely used a surname at this time. Meredith's name in Welsh was Maredudd ap Tudur, Meredith son of Tudor, Tudor being his father's first name. In order to distance himself from events in Wales Meredith altered his son's name from Owain ap Maredydd to Owen Tudor, giving Owen his grandfather's name as a surname. Had Owen not taken this step, we would later have been ruled by the Meredith dynasty.

Born around 1400, Owen was entered into service as a page to the King's Steward in the court of King Henry IV. In 1415 he fought at Agincourt for King Henry V after which he entered the service of Henry V's queen, Catherine of Valois. Following the death of Henry V he remained in the queen's service. Catherine now became something of an issue for the infant king's uncles who ruled in his name. She was a young French princess and likely to wish to marry again, but Humphrey of Gloucester, who acted as Protector, was concerned about the impact of a new husband and his possible influence on the young king. Catherine was likely to marry a foreign royal or perhaps a lower born English noble, so she was kept under close watch and a statute passed through Parliament forbidding anyone to marry a queen without the king's permission. The penalty for breach of this was forfeiture of land and possessions for life. With the king too young to offer any consent, it seemed Catherine was secured.

However, a secret affair ended in Catherine's marriage to her servant Owen Tudor. It is believed to have been a love match with a deep passion between them. Owen was a handsome young Welshman, Catherine a beautiful French princess. It also thwarted the legislation. Owen had no land or possessions to forfeit, so nothing to lose by marrying the queen.

In 1432, Owen applied to Parliament for naturalisation. Henry IV had robbed Welsh nationals of any rights after their rebellion and Owen tried to remove this obstacle, not least for his heirs. He was successful and it was around this time that Catherine gave birth to a son, Edmund, followed by Jasper, Owen and a daughter. By 1436, though, Catherine was gravely ill and died. Owen panicked that Humphrey of Gloucester would seek retribution now he was not protected and fled. The news of his mother's remarriage had also been kept from King Henry VI and Owen must have feared his reaction to the revelation too. He was captured and placed in Newgate jail, escaping only to be returned and then moved to the Tower of London. Released on bail in 1438, Owen was pardoned in 1439.

His sons Edmund and Jasper were placed with the de la Pole family. His namesake Owen entered the clergy. During the 1440's Henry VI took an interest in his half-brothers, perhaps as a link to his mother or because he did not yet have an heir of his own. In 1452 he created Edmund Earl and Richmond and Jasper Earl of Pembroke. Owen had lived to see two of his sons created belted English earls.

Lady Margaret Beaufort was placed into the care of Edmund and Jasper. Her inheritance was appealing and Edmund, as was his right, married Margaret when she was 12 and he 24 years old. It was not usual to consummate a marriage at this time below the age of 14, but Margaret was quickly pregnant. Edmund may have had a ruthless, cynical approach to this, since any child, whether they survived or not, would secure Margaret's inheritance for Edmund as the father, making the vast wealth and lands his permanently, not by virtue of his wife.

As the Wars of the Roses erupted, Edmund spent time incarcerated in Wales during which he contracted the plague, which was to kill him before his wife delivered her child. Margaret was taken into the care of her brother-in-law Jasper and delivered her son Henry Tudor on a stormy night on 29th January 1457 at Pembroke Castle. The birth was reportedly difficult and may have been the reason that she never conceived again and devoted all of her efforts to protecting her precious only son.

The Foundations of Conflict

King Henry VI was a man deeply unsuited to the position into which he was born. Henry became King of England on 31st August 1422 aged 9 months upon the death of his father, the glorious warrior-king Henry V. He was also heir to the French throne following his father's successes. His uncles were placed in charge of his territories during his long minority. Humphrey, Duke of Gloucester was Protector of the Realm in England, effectively ruling in Henry's name with the aid of a council. John, Duke of Bedford was made Regent of France and fought hard to maintain the infant's territories there. The French king died later that same year and his son was quickly crowned. In response, Henry was crowned King of France in Rouen.

His minority was ended in 1437 when Henry was declared to have come of age and took the reins of government. Henry emerged from his minority blinking into the dazzling light of a world for which he was ill prepared. He was pious, quiet and shy. Disliking war, bloodshed and the frivolity of court life, Henry began to favour peace with France. He was supported in this by Cardinal Beaufort and by William de la Pole, Earl of Suffolk. Hungry to continue pressing English claims in France were the king's uncle Humphrey, Duke of Gloucester and his most powerful subject Richard, Duke of York.

Cardinal Beaufort and the Earl of Suffolk prevailed and were instrumental in arranging Henry's marriage to Margaret of Anjou, a niece of King Charles VII of France. The Treaty of Tours was agreed but its key provisions were kept secret from Parliament. Henry had agreed to cede Maine and Anjou and not to receive a dowry for the marriage. The wedding took place on 23rd April 1445 and the territories were lost.

At this time two factions emerged at court and it was Henry's inability to resolve this conflict that set the foundations of civil war. On one side, William de la Pole, Earl of Suffolk, the now elderly statesman Cardinal Beaufort and his nephew Edmund Beaufort, now 2nd Duke of Somerset following the death of his brother John, had the favour of the king and, perhaps more importantly, his forceful queen. They sought peace with France and were securing significant patronage at court. Opposing them was Humphrey, Duke of Gloucester and Richard, Duke of York. Richard was Henry's heir presumptive until the king had a child and favoured hostility with France, resenting the increasing influence of Suffolk and Somerset.

In 1447, with the support of the king and queen, Suffolk and Somerset had Gloucester charged with treason. He was arrested and died in custody, possibly of a heart attack though rumours abounded that he had been poisoned. York was despatched to Ireland where he ruled for the king, gathering much support to the House of York but in little doubt that it was effectively exile. Suffolk was forced from favour by failures, including taking the blame for the costly marriage negotiations of the king and lawlessness in East Anglia. Banished for 5 years, his boat was attacked on the way to Calais. Suffolk was executed and his body thrown overboard. Rumour quickly circulated that York's long arms had arranged the attack. Somerset was given command in France and failed so completely that by 1453 only Calais remained in English hands.

1450 had seen an uprising in Kent that had stormed London. The rising has been titled Cade's Rebellion after its leader, Jack Cade, a shadowy figure often linked to the Duke of York. Among the rebels' demands was the return to court of the duke. The rebels stormed London and, having presented their demands, were assured that they would be met and all rebels would be pardoned. No demands were met and the rebel leaders, including Cade, were hunted down and executed. Although ultimately a failure, the rebellion shows the strength of the concerns that were growing around Henry VI's kingship and his choice of advisors. London admitted the rebels, primarily because they were sympathetic to their demands. It was also clear that the popular choice to right these perceived wrongs was Richard, Duke of York.

A Storm Gathers

In early 1453, Henry VI must have felt as though he had finally got the hang of being king. The previous year, York had risen with a force of men and marched on London. Protesting his loyalty to the king, York sought only to remove his councillors, particularly Somerset. The duke's army camped outside London and was approached by the Duke of Buckingham and the Earls of Salisbury and Warwick, York's brothers-in-law and nephew respectively. It is worth noting Warwick's initial loyalty to Henry VI as a prelude to his later fame. York was in a weak negotiating position, but agreed to disband his force if Somerset was arrested. When the news of the king's acceptance of these terms arrived, York set off with a handful of retainers to meet Henry.

On arriving in the king's presence, York was greeted by the sight of Somerset at the king's side. Apparently the queen had intervened to prevent his removal. Isolated from his army, York was forced to lead the procession back into London as though he were a prisoner. He swore an oath of allegiance to Henry and promised never again to rise against the king's person with an armed force. Suitably cowed, he was released, withdrawing to Ludlow and effective exile from court once again.

To add to Henry's mounting optimism, after 7 years of marriage, his wife Margaret was pregnant. It seemed that uncertainty over the succession may be resolving itself favourably. The previous year, Henry had also made a confident about-face and opened hostilities with France, hoping to emulate his father. Still to come were the terrible losses of all territory but Calais. In November 1452, Henry created his half-brothers, Edmund and Jasper Tudor, Earls of Richmond and Pembroke respectively. Edmund swiftly married Margaret Beaufort with the king's approval. Margaret, the niece of the current Duke of Somerset, was the wealthiest heiress in England and the union cemented the Tudor brothers within the Lancastrian establishment and gave Henry fiercely loyal allies. Peace at home and war with France made for a happy kingdom.

As the middle of 1453 approached, though, Henry's confidence and his attachment to Edmund Beaufort, Duke of Somerset were to cost him dearly. Henry spent the early months of the year touring his kingdom, settling local disputes and showing himself to his subjects. In July, he returned to Greenwich and was met by a problem. Somerset was engaged in a rapidly escalating dispute with Richard Neville, Earl of Warwick. Warwick's father was the Earl of Salisbury, his aunt was Cecily Neville, wife of the Duke of York and the dispute concerned a matrimonial inheritance in Wales. Upon the death of his father-in-law, Warwick had been granted half of the Despenser inheritance of his father-in-law's last wife. Warwick had held these lands since 1450 but for reasons best known to Henry, he had placed custody of the Despenser lands into the hands of Somerset. Given Warwick's previous loyalty, he may have expected the matter to be resolved in his favour but when Council met at Sheen at the end of July, he was ordered to hand the lands over to Somerset. To compound matters, Somerset was present at Council to plead his case. Warwick was not.

Warwick seethed and dug in at Cardiff castle. Somerset set about evicting him. Henry left London, heading for Dorset to settle the matter in person. Near Salisbury, at the royal hunting lodge at Clarendon, matters took an unexpected turn. Just before leaving London, news had reached Henry of his army's defeat at Castillon which effectively lost all English territory in France apart from Calais. Messengers also brought tales of a renewed Neville-Percy feud in the north that was threatening to spill over into conflict. Perhaps the combination of all of these setbacks after riding such an unaccustomed high, added to the Valois blood that flowed in Henry's veins, the blood of the mad French king Charles VI, undid the king. At the age of 31, Henry slipped into a catatonic state. The Abbot of St Albans, John Whethamstede wrote how 'a disease and disorder of such a sort overcame the king that he lost his wits and memory for a time, and nearly all his body was so uncoordinated and out of control that he could neither walk nor hold his head up, nor easily move from where he sat'.

The consequences of a king suddenly left incapacitated were seismic. No one could be sure how long his condition would persist. In the short term Council was able to maintain government and keep Henry's condition secret, but it lacked authority without the king. There was a gaping vacuum at the very centre of power and two bitter enemies seeking to fill it.

Protector and Defender of the Realm

Margaret gave birth to a son on 13th October 1453. Edward was named after his father's favourite saint, Edward the Confessor, but his birth, rather than resolving any burning issues, poured fuel upon the fire. First the Duke of Buckingham and then Queen Margaret herself presented the baby to the king. According to the Paston letters, Henry did not offer 'any answer or countenance, saving only that he looked on the Prince and cast his eyes down again without any more'. This was a serious development. By law, the baby was not Henry's legitimate son nor his heir until the king acknowledged him officially. Without Henry's acceptance of his son, there was still no heir, nothing to fill the vacuum. Worse still, rumour sprang up that the king had not accepted the child because it was, in fact, Somerset's child with Margaret. All of this had to end.

In January 1454, Queen Margaret made an audacious play to secure the position of her son. John Paston recorded that Margaret informed Council that she 'desireth to have the whole rule of this land'. Doubtless a bid to protect the positions of herself, her son and her favourite Somerset, her demands were a step too far for the misogynistic ruling class. If they would not tolerate Margaret to hold the king's power, they had only one other choice. Support and power trickled through the fingers of Queen Margaret and into the hands of the Duke of York. In February, Council nominated York as King's Lieutenant so that he could call a meeting of Parliament. Lines were drawn with Somerset frantically trying to assemble support on one side and York attracting powerful men to the other. The Earl of Warwick and his large private army were now firmly on the side of York. The king had seen to that before becoming incapacitated.

On 22th March, John Kemp died. He was the Archbishop of Canterbury and a new appointment to this vital role could only be made by the king. Members of Council visited the king to measure his condition. Finding him unchanged, they sent for the Duke of York. On 27th March 1454, Richard, Duke of York was created Protector and Defender of the Realm to act much as Humphrey, Duke of Gloucester had done during Henry's minority. Somerset was arrested and taken to the Tower. Margaret was placed under house arrest at Windsor. Some of the nobility waited in fear of the vengeance York was likely to unleash.

It is perhaps therefore remarkable that York's protectorate is generally considered a success. He greatly reduced the size of the royal household and their expenditure. With a decisive show of force he ended the Neville-Percy feud that was raging in the north. Although he did make key appointments within his own supporters, that is perhaps to be expected. In all other matters, he acted with equity and honour. The terms of his Protectorate made him subordinate still to King Henry and provided for him to exercise power until Henry's (still unrecognised) son was of age; potentially fourteen years ahead.

If King Henry's illness was a national crisis, his recovery was to prove a catastrophe. On 25th December 1454, Henry was restored as swiftly as he had been struck down. There was rejoicing. A few days later, when it seemed Henry had truly returned to himself, he was to provide an insight into the extent of his detachment over the past eighteen months. He had no recollection of his son, or of even having a son, yet in finally acknowledging young Edward, at a stroke he demonstrated his recovery and settled the long standing issue of the succession. On 30th December, York handed back all of his authority. Henry revoked many of York's appointments. Margaret was freed, along with Somerset who was restored as Captain of Calais (a vital title York had taken for his own) and Constable of England. York, along with Salisbury and Warwick, retired once more to his estates and pondered Somerset's treatment of the last Protector, the king's uncle Humphrey. Henry's return favoured the Percy family again, causing Warwick to consider his family's position. His father, Salisbury, was removed from his offices at court and must have known that the political wilderness beckoned for as long as Henry was king. Tension was tighter than a drawn bow string and conflict all but inevitable.

Civil War

England was doomed to what was to become over thirty years of strife and open warfare that fluctuated yet was rarely far from the surface. For the purposes of this book, the Wars of the Roses are separated into five key periods of conflict, but in reality the tensions, family loyalties and personal animosities that towed the nation from battlefield to battlefield for three decades were always at play. Dynastic conflict on a national scale was often the scene for the settling of personal, local disputes.

Ancient families had more to consider than who was king. They had proud traditions and a great deal to lose, beyond even their lives, by making a decision that would prove less than fortuitous. The choice between honour and right, loyalty and survival was stark and constantly being forced upon them.

For ordinary men and women, it is hard to measure the impact of conflicts such as the Wars of the Roses upon them. Those who served a lord heavily involved may have lived for years in constant fear of being called to battle. Families deprived of a husband and father would no doubt have struggled to make ends meet. If an army of either side was in the area, they would most likely devour food and drink on an unsustainable scale, threatening local supplies. They may, if in a hurry or even just unconcerned, march through fields of crops destroying harvests.

Henry Tudor, once king, paid substantial compensation to regions his army marched through, ruining crops.

For the most part, though, assuming conflict remained at a distance, it is likely that most were primarily concerned with securing enough food and money for them and their families, a more immediate concern than the disputes of great men.

The First Period

Wounds Opened

The opening battle of the Wars of the Roses was the First Battle of St Albans which took place on 22nd May 1455 within the town of St Albans. King Henry VI personally led his army. His commanders were Edmund Beaufort, Duke of Somerset and Humphrey Stafford, Duke of Buckingham. Henry's army numbered around 2,500 whilst Richard, Duke of York led a force around 3,000 strong. With the duke were the Earls of Salisbury and Warwick.

King Henry took a position in the market place. Wearing full armour and standing beneath the royal standard, he made himself easy to mark. Hostilities began in the mid morning and initially the king's forces held back the attacking Yorkists. The Earl of Warwick then instructed his archers to concentrate their fire on those protecting the king and bodies soon began to pile up in the market place. King Henry himself was struck in the neck by an arrow and ushered into a nearby building for treatment.

Foot soldiers moved in to complete the work of the archers, focussing their attack on the leaders of Henry's Lancastrian forces. Somerset fell fighting in the streets, as did Henry Percy, Earl of Northumberland. Thomas de Clifford was another notable casualty because his death was to prove the opening of the kind of wound that was to fester rather than heal over this period. His son swore that his father's death would not go unavenged. Around a hundred of the king's men fell, mostly men of note. Ordinary soldiers were generally spared.

Henry was quickly surrounded by the Yorkist leaders who immediately fell to their knees and professed their allegiance to him. Comforted, he spent the night at St Albans Abbey, though he was reportedly devastated at the news of the death of Somerset. The battle was swift and casualties few, though distinguished. The consequences of St Albans were far reaching. Henry was still king but was firmly under York's control.

Possibly as a result of the stress of his injuries and the losses suffered, Henry slipped into another period of catatonia. York was reinstalled as Protector. Warwick, significantly, was appointed Captain of Calais. Although it was common at the time to appoint a deputy to oversee the role, Warwick decided to move to Calais himself. Once more, York was even handed in his running of the government.

Meanwhile, the queen began to gather about her those whose hatred of York made them keen allies. Amongst those gravitating toward her were Henry Beaufort, Somerset's son and successor as Duke of Somerset, Henry Percy the new Earl of Northumberland, the king's half-brother Jasper Tudor, Earl of Pembroke, and the son of Thomas de Clifford. Although Henry's court was living beyond its income,

Margaret viewed York's reduction of her household and expenditure as aggressive. She came to view him as a threat not only to her husband but to her young son. Queen Margaret believed York wanted the throne.

On 25th February 1456 Henry appeared before Parliament to receive York's resignation of his position. The king was restored once more, though none knew for how long. With Somerset gone, Henry appeared keen to keep York close, retaining him on the Council. York had proved himself a steady hand upon the tiller and Henry's recovery was an unknown quantity to all, including Henry, in terms of its extent and duration. Warwick was confirmed as Captain of Calais, perhaps not least because it kept him out of the country.

Although the first period of conflict appears brief, it established that armed rising against the king was no longer inconceivable. Indeed, such a coup had been successful. As dangerous as this precedent was, the queen's concern that it should not happen again was just as divisive. Even with Somerset gone, two sides still remained and animosity still smouldered.

This first period drew to a close with a Love Day celebrated in London on the Feast Day of the Annunciation, 24th March 1458. To demonstrate the healed wounds, King Henry processed wearing his crown followed by York and the queen holding hands. Behind them were Salisbury and Somerset side by side. The line continued, with rivals pushed together and obliged to smile as though all was well. No doubt King Henry believed that it was. His condition left him with little interest in politics and he spent much of his time sleeping or in prayer. The procession was not one of healed wounds. It was a bandage covering festering sores and the bandage was about to fall off.

The Second Period

Battle Lines

An uneasy peace was endured for four years after St Albans but by 1459, tensions were no longer bearable and both Queen Margaret and the Duke of York began openly arming themselves and gathering their forces in readiness for conflict. York established a base at Ludlow. The castle was strong, highly defensible and lay in Yorkist territory. The royal forces began to gather around Coventry.

The first engagement took place at the Battle of Blore Heath on 23rd September 1459 near Market Drayton in Staffordshire. The Earl of Salisbury had gathered his northern forces from the Neville lands and was marching to meet York at Ludlow with around 5,000 men. Hearing of the movement, the queen despatched Lord Audley with 10,000 men to intercept Salisbury. The move was sound - the Yorkist forces were dispersed and isolated. Warwick had only just landed on the south coast with his Calais garrison. The royal force outnumbered Salisbury 2:1.

When it became clear that the way was blocked, Salisbury's army took a defensive position between a wood and their supply wagons with a brook between them and the enemy. Although shallow, the banks of the brook were steep and the approach required Audley's forces to move uphill, a tiring task. When

Audley sent in the first charge, Salisbury's experienced archers sent a hail of arrows down upon them. Men at arms then waded in to finish off the rest. A second charge was launched with the same result. Lord Audley led the third charge and died attempting to reach Salisbury's position. It is said that the brook ran red for three days after the slaughter.

Salisbury continued on to Ludlow and was joined there a few days later by his son Warwick. York was already there with his eldest sons Edward, Earl of March and Edmund, Earl of Rutland. Their force now numbered perhaps 20-25,000 men. News arrived though that the royal army was approaching and was twice the size of the Yorkist force. Most of the nobility outside the clique gathered at Ludlow remained loyal to their king. Significantly, even frighteningly, the army was being led by King Henry himself under the royal standard. This changed the game altogether.

The Yorkists sent letters to the king protesting their loyalty to him. Henry sent back a promise of pardons for any who would abandon York's cause now. Salisbury was excluded from the pardon for his part in the slaughter at Blore Heath. As evening approached on 11th October 1459, York's army dug trenches and earth walls around their position at Ludgate Meadows just outside the town. The royal standard visible in the near distance was to prove too much.

To the mediaeval mind, taking the field of battle against the enemies of your liege lord in some dispute was part and parcel of life. To take up arms against

God's anointed king was a whole different matter. Aside from treason, it was considered a mortal sin. Dying in battle was one thing, but risking your soul was not something a mediaeval man or woman could ever do. So, in leading the army personally, Henry VI decided the battle before it began.

The leader of the Calais force brought by Warwick was Sir Andrew Trollope. A noted soldier, he had served with Henry V in France and although obliged to Warwick, appeared to have no intention of taking the field against his former leader's son, the anointed king. The Calais garrison scaled the earthworks and fled into the night and the king's waiting pardon.

An emergency council of war was held within Ludlow Castle and the leaders took possibly the only sensible route open to them. York and his son Edmund fled to Ireland whilst his other son Edward accompanied Salisbury and Warwick to the south coast and made for the security of Calais. York's wife Cecily and his other children, including his younger sons George and Richard, were left inside Ludlow Castle. Possibly attempting to save the town, Cecily is said to have met the king's army the next morning standing at the market cross with her two sons. Richard must have been terrified at 7 years old and no doubt the incident left its mark.

If Cecily intended to save the town, she did not. The royal army fell upon Ludlow like a conquered French town. They drank, robbed and raped until they were sated, looting the castle of anything of value too. Cecily and her children were placed into the care of her sister, Humphrey Stafford's wife, the Duchess of Buckingham.

June 1460 saw the beginning of a year of conflict that escalated to terrifying proportions. Salisbury, Warwick and March landed on the south coast and set about besieging the Tower of London. Warwick marched his forces north to meet the royal army that was leaving Coventry to support London. The two armies met at the Battle of Northampton on 10th July with the royal army holding a defensive position. The battle turned upon the defection of Lord Grey who switched to Warwick's side and attacked the king's army leading to a decisive Yorkist victory. King Henry was captured. Amongst the royalist casualties was Humphrey Stafford, Duke of Buckingham.

With Henry firmly under the control of his faction, the Duke of York returned to England and London, this time making no secret of his desire to claim the throne for himself. Having frequently pledged his allegiance to Henry, this breach of honour was not well received. He failed to secure enough support and Henry refused to abdicate. Stalemate ensued with none amongst the political establishment willing to provide a decision, thereby upsetting either the king or his mightiest subject. Finally, on 8th November the Act of Accord provided that Richard, Duke of York should be heir to King Henry and that York and his heirs would rule upon Henry's death.

The queen would not stomach an arrangement that disinherited her son. The battle for the throne was begun in earnest. In December, York set out with his son Edmund and the Earl of Salisbury to meet the threat of a large Lancastrian force assembling at York. With around 8,000 men, York was horrified to find about 18,000 mustered against him under the leadership of Henry Beaufort, Duke of Somerset, Henry Holland, Duke of Exeter, Henry Percy, Earl of Northumberland and Lord Clifford. York fell back to Sandal Castle to await reinforcements from his eldest son Edward.

For reasons that are not known for certain, York led his army out of the security of the castle to engage the larger Lancastrian force before support arrived. It is possible that he was taunted into battle. If so, his pride was to be his undoing. York fell during the fighting. His son Edmund was captured in the rout as was Salisbury. Both were beheaded. It is said that Lord Clifford personally killed the seventeen year old Edmund as he pleaded for mercy, fulfilling his pledge to avenge his father. York's corpse was unceremoniously sat upon an anthill with a paper crown on his head and taunted. He too was then beheaded. All three heads were set upon spikes on Micklegate Bar at the entrance to York. Wounds opened at St Albans now bled freely.

When Edward heard of the defeat and death of his father, brother and uncle, he headed east toward London to join Warwick. En route he received word of a Lancastrian force crossing Wales and moved to meet them. Edward's 11,000 men outnumbered the 8,000 led by Jasper Tudor, Earl of Pembroke and James Butler, Earl of Wiltshire. Edward won the battle of Mortimer's Cross on 2nd February 1461, routing the Lancastrians. The most notable casualty of this engagement was the 60 year old Welshman Owen Tudor, father of Edmund and Jasper and grandfather of the future King Henry VII.

On 17th February, Warwick was at St Albans awaiting Edward's victorious army. Denying him the luxury of time, the Lancastrians led by the Duke of Somerset attacked. Although the forces were about even, each numbering around 25,000 men, Warwick fled when the Second Battle of St Albans did not go his way. He left the captive King Henry sat under a tree in his hurry to escape.

Edward proclaimed himself King Edward IV on 4th March 1461 and set about crushing the Lancastrians. On 28th March the Battle of Ferrybridge saw Yorkist forces rally having been almost defeated by the Lancastrians but this was a prelude to the culmination of the open warfare of this period. Many of the nobility and gentry had been wiped out by the wars. The past two years had seen battle after battle, no one side winning successive victories. The omens may have been poor for King Edward as he met the Lancastrian army in the final, cataclysmic struggle of this period.

The Battle of Towton on 29th March 1461 is remembered as the bloodiest battle ever to take place on English soil. 36,000 Yorkist men faced 40,000 Lancastrians in the driving snow. Yorkist archers used the wind to their advantage, increasing their range beyond that of their enemy. In response, the Lancastrians charged. The larger Lancastrian force had the upper hand until John Mowbray, Duke of Norfolk arrived to reinforce the Yorkists. By the end of the day Edward was victorious. Henry, Margaret and their son fled to Scotland. The scale of the battle was unprecedented and an estimate 28,000 Englishmen lay dead, killed by Englishmen. Amongst them were Henry Percy, Earl of Northumberland and Sir Andrew Trollope of the Calais garrison.

Edward returned to London and was finally crowned King Edward IV at Westminster on 28th June 1461. He had defeated the Lancastrian king and placed the House of York upon the throne, completing his father's work. Towton marked the end of the second period of the Wars of the Roses and ushered in a period of relative peace and prosperity. Yet Edward had failed to secure the old king and he could not yet feel safe.

The Third Period

Insurgence

The third period of conflict was brief and demonstrated both the dominance of the Yorkist King Edward and the desperation of his Lancastrian opponents. In April 1464, three years into his rule, Edward sent Warwick's brother John Neville to negotiate peace with Scottish envoys on the border. On the way, Neville was ambushed by a force of around 5,000 Lancastrians led by Somerset. At the Battle of Hedgeley Moor on 25th April 1464, the forces were of equal size but both Lancastrian wings, commanded by Lords Hungerford and Roos, fled during the battle and the remaining force was quickly defeated. Somerset escaped and led what was left of his army south to Hexham.

At Hexham, Somerset was rejoined by Hungerford and Roos and his force again numbered around 5,000 men. After the completion of his diplomatic mission, John marched on Hexham to deal with the Lancastrians. On 15th May, taking the high ground, Neville's forces charged head long down the hill and swept away the Lancastrian force. Somerset, Hungerford and Roos were all captured and executed. Thus at the Battle of Hexham armed resistance to Edward was eradicated and, although still at large,

Henry and Margaret were isolated and without support.

The kingdom settled into relative peace. Edward was young, athletic and tall. At 6'4" he is the tallest King of England known to date, an inch taller than his grandson, Henry VIII. With harmony came prosperity. Trade improved and Edward worked hard to reconcile former Lancastrians to his rule. The next phase of trouble was to tear the kingdom apart afresh, exposing enemies Edward could not have expected.

Perhaps the primary cause of the troubles to come was King Edward's new queen. On 14th September 1464 Edward announced to a meeting of his Council that he had, a few months previously, married in secret. Furthermore, he had married a commoner, a widow four years his elder who had two sons from her first marriage. That first marriage also happened to have been to a prominent Lancastrian knight who had been killed at the Second Battle of St Albans. The Council could scarcely have imagined a worse match. French chronicler Jean de Waurin wrote that the Council told Edward 'he must know she was no wife for a prince such as himself'.

One man took particular offence at the match. The Earl of Warwick was close to concluding negotiations with France for Edward to marry the king's daughter, bringing peace between the countries. Edward's announcement caused him embarrassment at home and abroad that he would not bear lightly. The Earl would earn his title Kingmaker soon, primarily because of the king's marriage to Elizabeth Woodville.

The Woodvilles

There is a reason that the Woodville family were not included with the great families of the day at the beginning of this book. That reason is simple. They were not a great family. Neither, though, were they commoners in the sense that the accusation is usually levelled at them. Sir Richard Woodville (or Wydeville as it is sometimes spelt) was chamberlain to John, Duke of Bedford, the brother of King Henry V who acted as Regent of France whilst Henry VI was a child. After John died in 1435, Sir Richard's son, another Richard, married the widowed duchess. This Richard had been born in 1405 and had fought in France for the Duke of Bedford, serving under Somerset and York.

The marriage of the widowed Duchess Jacquetta of Luxembourg to a man of such comparatively low birth was a scandal at the time. The couple kept their relationship secret for a while but were fined when it came to light. In order to make the match more palatable, Richard was created Baron Rivers by Henry VI in 1448. In 1450 he was made a Knight of the Garter and in 1459 was appointed Warden of the Cinque Ports. A Lancastrian at the outbreak of fighting, Rivers was captured by Warwick and hauled to Calais. There, William Paston wrote, before Warwick, Salisbury and March he was publically berated 'that his father was but a squire'. Apparently 'my Lord of March rated him in like wise'. Awkward as an introduction to a future father-in-law.

Baron Rivers and his wife had 13 children in total. Elizabeth was the eldest and in 1452 she married Sir John Grey of Groby, heir to the Barony of Groby. The couple had two sons before Sir John's death, Thomas Grey, later Marquess of Dorset (from who Lady Jane Grey, the Nine Days Queen was descended) and Richard Grey. Elizabeth was widowed after the Second Battle of St Albans in 1461 but three years later caught the eye of the king and the couple married in secret.

The nature of their courtship is unclear. It has been speculated that Elizabeth refused the king's advances in order to preserve her reputation. She supposedly told Edward that if she was too lowly to be his wife, she was too high to be his mistress. Whether she did or not, Edward was so infatuated that he asked her to become his wife, not his mistress. Doubtless aware of the reaction they could expect, the union was kept secret for several months. When exposed, the political establishment reacted badly.

Nevertheless, Elizabeth went on to provide the king with several children, including two sons. Her siblings were given advantageous marriages by virtue of their sister's new position. Her brother Anthony succeeded his father, becoming the 2nd Earl Rivers. He was a learned man who performed very well in tournaments to the pleasure of his brother-in-law. Her sister Catherine married Henry Stafford, Duke of

Buckingham, Mary married into the Herbert family becoming Countess of Pembroke and her brother Lionel became Bishop of Salisbury to name but three.

The Woodvilles were viewed with distain by the nobility. They were seen as social pariahs, collecting the most profitable unions and offices at court. No doubt much of this dislike stemmed from jealousy. The Woodvilles held great influence and that was to the detriment of others. Their thrust for position and possession is, however, entirely to be expected and is indeed justified as the family of the Queen of England. Yet they certainly made enemies that would never be reconciled.

Kingmaker, Kingbreaker

The emergence of the Woodville family not only embarrassed Warwick as he sought a French marriage but also threatened his position as the king's senior subject. Warwick had secured the north, ending Percy dominance and quieting the Scottish borders. He disliked the way in which Edward had treated him, excluding him from such a vital decision, embarrassing him, creasing his honour and providing an unspoken yet clear threat to the Neville family's ascendancy. Warwick felt that he, in no small way, had made Edward king and he did not appreciate the way in which he was being repaid. In something of a sulk, Warwick retreated to his estates.

In 1465, Henry, who had been on the run since the Battle of Hexham, was discovered in the home of a Lancastrian sympathiser. Taken to London, he was paraded through the streets on 24th June as proof of his capture. He was then securely installed within the Tower of London where he was to spend the next five years as a comfortable, possibly bewildered, prisoner. Margaret and their son Edward were still at large and Edward possibly preferred to keep Henry alive as a limp Lancastrian figurehead rather than reinvigorate the line by removing Henry and making his son, the young and fit Edward, the new Lancastrian hope.

Warwick still seethed. He began to throw ostentatious parties, banquets that were always one course longer and more extravagant than the king's. He was flexing his muscles in response to Edward's treatment of him. Warwick favoured an allegiance with France but the Woodvilles preferred a Burgundian treaty. Edward tended to agree, marrying his sister Margaret to the widowed Charles of Burgundy, heir to Duke Philip. As part of the negotiations, Edward also sought to marry his brother George, Duke of Clarence to Charles's daughter Mary. Warwick had already sought to arrange a marriage between George and his own eldest daughter, Isabel. Edward forbade the union on the grounds that the couple were first cousins once removed and would hear no more on the matter. Warwick was being squeezed further from influence.

When a Burgundian delegation arrived in 1467 for a tournament to decide the Champion of Europe between Anthony Woodville and Antony, Bastard of Burgundy, Warwick's brother George Neville, Chancellor and Archbishop of York refused to attend. In response to the snub, Edward stripped George of his office. Warwick, who had been on a diplomatic mission to France, returned with a French delegation, which was roundly ignored, to learn of his brother's disgrace.

In Wales, an insurrection flared in 1468, funded by the affronted and mischievous King Louis of France. Jasper Tudor led the assault in the name of Henry's son, the Prince of Wales. William, Lord Herbert led King Edward's response, crushing the rebellion and forcing Jasper to flee disguised as a peasant. Lord Herbert's reward was the grant of Jasper's own title, Earl of Pembroke. Herbert was a staunch Yorkist loyalist. From an established Welsh family, he had married Mary Woodville, one of the queen's sisters, and began to accrue lands in England now too. Another upon whom Edward came to rely and to lavish patronage, Warwick felt his previously short path to the heart of power extending beyond his reach.

It is hard to pinpoint the precise reason that Warwick's disenchantment evolved into opposition. It is most likely the steady accumulation of snubs and knock-backs along with watching his own hard won influence wane. During 1468, a series of Lancastrian plots were exposed seeking to reinstate Henry VI and Warwick perhaps saw this willing opposition to the charismatic king as his opportunity. On 11th July 1469, Warwick married his eldest daughter Isabel to George, Duke of Clarence. Although Edward had forbidden the union and consanguinity required Papal dispensation, the match was made, with Warwick's brother, the Archbishop of York presiding. It is interesting that the marriage took place with the necessary permission from Rome. After Edward had prohibited the match, Warwick had secretly continued to lobby in Rome for the dispensation; an early suggestion that dissent was on his mind.

Almost immediately after the wedding, Warwick issued a list of complaints aimed at the king's advisors, a now ominously familiar ploy. He had seen a chink and meant to exploit it. Edward had dared to underestimate Warwick's worth, he had forgotten who had put him upon his throne and the earl was going to remind him. Although he would not acquire the Kingmaker epithet until long after his death, Warwick was playing the part again. Spreading rumours about Edward's legitimacy, Warwick's aim was to place George upon the throne, with his own daughter Isabel as queen.

The Fourth Period

Rise and Fall

In April 1469, a small uprising was swiftly subdued by John Neville, Earl of Northumberland, brother of Warwick. John had acquired the earldom following the Percy family's disgrace and was loyal to Edward. The rebellion did not die though and a list of grievances was circulated that bore a striking resemblance to those wounding Warwick's pride. The rebels wanted the pernicious Woodville family removed from power. The rebel leader was identified as Robin of Redesdale, Robin being a standard name by this time for a rebel seeking to right wrongs for the people's benefit. Although his identity is not known for certain, it has been suggested that Robin of Redesdale was, in fact, Sir William Conyers, a Neville family ally. Whoever he really was, it seems likely that Warwick was the instigator.

Confident of crushing the uprising, King Edward raised a small force and began to march north to meet them. When the scale of the insurrection became clear, Edward turned back to wait for reinforcements at Nottingham. William Herbert, Earl of Pembroke and Humphrey Stafford, Earl of Devon were called upon to assist. Stafford was a distant relative of the Earls of Stafford and owned a large portion of land in the south west of England.

The smoke screen created by this uprising covered the landing of Warwick and Clarence on the south coast. They made their way through Kent and men flocked to Warwick's banner. The earl was immensely popular and Kent, it seems, was always ready to rise. With a swelling force, they made their way north to join the rebels. When the northern rebels attempted to bypass the king's army and meet Warwick, they ran into the reinforcements of Pembroke and Devon near Banbury in Oxfordshire.

The two royal armies had camped a distance apart on 25th July and the rebels took the opportunity to attack Pembroke on the morning of 26th whilst Devon and his force of Welsh archers were several miles away. Pembroke was forced back until Devon arrived to assist, but at the same moment, Warwick's army arrived to reinforce the rebels. Pembroke's men took flight at the spectacle of Warwick's liveried professionals taking the field. Pembroke himself was captured and executed the following day, Devon sharing his fate a few days later. The Battle of Edgecote Moor had reignited the Wars of the Roses.

Immediately after the battle, George Neville, Archbishop of York took the king into his custody and delivered the prize to his brother, Warwick. Richard Woodville, Earl Rivers and his son John were captured and executed also. Warwick had taken a measure of revenge upon the upstarts who had barred his door to power. King Edward was kept as Warwick's prisoner until September of 1469 when it became all but impossible to rule without the person of the king. Warwick was forced to release Edward.

An uneasy peace was endured for several months between the king and his mightiest subject, but then Edward chose to send a very clear message to the earl. John Neville had held the Earldom of Northumberland since 1465, but the late Percy Earl's son Henry had sworn fealty to King Edward and petitioned for the return of his paternal inheritance. In a move either self destructive or by its design instructive to Warwick, Edward agreed to Henry Percy's restoration. John Neville was forced to quit the title and lands of the Earldom of Northumberland in favour of the Neville family's bitter and disgraced rivals. Edward was seeking to demonstrate to his erstwhile controller just who held the reins of power. John was created Marquess of Montagu by way of compensation, but the title was a clear demotion and left John with a much depleted income and pride as bruised as that of his brother. John's son George Neville was created Duke of Bedford and promised a match with King Edward's eldest daughter Elizabeth of York. If the king thought that he had appeased Montagu, he was sorely mistaken.

In March 1470, unrest in Lincolnshire erupted into open conflict when Richard, Lord Welles, second cousin to Warwick, attacked the manor of Sir Thomas Burgh, Master of the King's Horse. Edward decided to intervene personally. Lord Welles was summoned to London to explain himself but in his absence, his son

Robert raised a fresh rebellion. King Edward raised a force and headed north to meet them. The two forces met on 12th March 1470 at Empingham. As a demonstration of the king's resolve, Lord Welles was executed in front of Edward's army before fighting began. The Lincolnshire rebels panicked at the sight of the king's army and fled. In their hurry to escape and perhaps to avoid identification, many shed their surcoats and the battle became known as the Battle of Losecote Field.

Edward stood victorious upon the battlefield, his dominance reasserted. A week later, Robert Welles was executed, though not before he had confessed his part in full and implicated both Warwick and Clarence in the plot. Documents were also supposedly found detailing the extent of Warwick and Clarence's involvement. The earl and duke had stalked Edward north with an army of their own, hoping to trap the king once more. When Welles' force was routed, they turned back, fleeing to France when it became clear that they had been exposed.

A tragic episode ensued as Lord Wenlock, who controlled Calais in Warwick's absence, refused to allow his old master to dock. Edward had ordered Wenlock to deny them entry and he did so. Sadly, Isabel was with her husband and was nine months pregnant. Even as she went into labour, they were denied permission to land and although Isabel survived, the duke and duchess's first child, a daughter, was stillborn. Burgundy also prevented

Warwick from landing within their territory and they were forced to eventually make port at Honfleur in France.

The Bear And The She-Wolf

King Louis XI of France acquired the nickname 'The Universal Spider' for his delicate political web weaving. He knew his enemies well and was always keen to make mischief for them. During their earlier negotiations, it appears that Louis had taken a liking to Warwick and he now saw a chance to promote the Lancastrian cause of Margaret of Anjou, if only he could reconcile these two most bitter of enemies. Margaret had been dubbed a 'She-Wolf' for her aggressive nature. Warwick's badge was the bear and ragged staff. Louis now sought to ensnare these two wounded animals in his latest web. Somehow, he managed to convince them of their common cause - perhaps advising them that the enemy of their enemy was the only friend that they had.

Warwick and Margaret met in mid July at Angers. Warwick got down on bended knee to pledge his loyalty to Margaret. She in turn made him stay there for over a quarter of an hour before agreeing to an alliance with the man who had aided in removing her husband's crown. Warwick was promised men and funds if he were to put the Lancastrians back upon the throne. Margaret was no doubt told that whatever she may think of him, Warwick represented her and her son's last chance of a return to England. Once restored, the Lancastrians were to assist Louis in cowing Burgundy as he sought to subsume all of the independent Duchies that ringed France. To seal the alliance, Warwick's younger daughter Anne was to be married to Edward of Westminster, son and heir to Henry VI and Margaret, imbedding Warwick's Neville blood within the royal family. Everyone was set to win, except Edward, and one other person.

One of Warwick's brothers-in-law sparked fresh unrest in the north. Edward, recognising the success of Losecote Field, decided to act personally and decisively once again. He marched north and the uprising evaporated, its instigator fleeing over the border to Scotland. By early September 1469, Edward was on his way south again, stopping in the Midlands. Meanwhile, Warwick had landed on the south coast, accompanied by Clarence, John de Vere, Earl of Oxford (another brother-in-law to Warwick) and Jasper Tudor who was seeking restoration of his own Earldom of Pembroke. The support that flowed to the charismatic Warwick was now swelled further by Lancastrian loyalists, emboldened to show their hand. The force grew daily as it marched north to depose King Edward and restore King Henry. The north was traditionally Lancastrian and was, too, made brave by the resurgent fortunes of that House. The final straw was the defection of Montagu to his brother's side. He had not forgiven Edward and now meant to seize him. Edward was caught between a hammer and the anvil and took the only step open to him - a sideways one. Riding to Kings Lyn, he procured a ship and on the 2nd October 1469 he fled to his sister Margaret and brother-in-law, Charles, Duke of Burgundy.

Taking ship alongside their king were Anthony Woodville, now Earl Rivers, Lord Hastings, a close personal friend and advisor to Edward and his young brother Richard, Duke of Gloucester. The date that they boarded the ship to flee into exile was, in fact, Richard's eighteenth birthday. In light of their brother George, Duke of Clarence's betrayal, Richard's loyalty at this point was to set the benchmark for the next fourteen years. Richard had been raised in Warwick's household, mainly at Middleham Castle in Yorkshire. As was traditional, he had been placed in the care of a senior noble for his education and training. It is conceivable, or perhaps even likely, that Warwick sought to recruit Richard to his cause too. Whether he did or not, the young duke stood with his brother and other steadfast Yorkists as they sailed for Burgundy and began to plan their return.

Henry was released from the Tower of London and proclaimed the rightful king, termed his 'readeption to royal power'. It was clear, though, that Henry was a puppet in the proceedings. It was also clear that this suited Warwick perfectly. Lancastrians emerging from hiding traded places with Yorkists who sank into the shadows. The only significant Yorkist executed was John Tiptoft, Earl of Worcester, possibly a personal revenge for his previous hanging, drawing and quartering of twenty of Warwick's supporters. Elizabeth Woodville took sanctuary in Westminster

Abbey where she was to give birth to a son, named for his absent father. Edward and Richard were disinherited and Warwick set about ruling in Henry's name.

All seemed to be going well. Henry was greeted rapturously. Warwick was named Protector of the Realm and Great Chamberlain of England. He also took back the Captaincy of Calais. Jasper Tudor regained his earldom, riding to Hereford to take custody of his young nephew Henry Tudor from William Herbert's widow. Parliament confirmed Henry as king, Prince Edward as his heir and, should that line fail, George, Duke of Clarence was to succeed. In the meantime, Clarence became Lord Lieutenant of Ireland. Still, given that their original aim was to place Clarence upon the throne, the haughty duke may have viewed this settlement as unsatisfactory. He was viewed with caution by Lancastrians, wary of the exiled former king's brother, yet simultaneously seen as a traitor by Yorkists. His position was precarious and he was growing isolated.

Two Kings, One Crown

The beginning of 1471 saw Edward gathering support from Burgundy, now under attack from France with English aid promised, while Margaret of Anjou and her son prepared to leave France and return to England. Margaret delayed, spending Christmas 1470 in Paris and then awaiting Warwick's arrival to escort her to England. Warwick protested that lack of funds made the journey impossible and whilst this is probably true - he had spent heavily to see Henry returned to the throne and, without a source of tax revenue, was personally funding the royal household - it is also possible that he viewed Margaret's return with the Prince of Wales as a threat to his own position.

While Margaret prevaricated, Edward left Burgundy with a small force of just over a thousand men. Having attempted to land at Cromer and finding no welcome, Edward skirted the east coast until storms that further delayed Margaret's departure swept his fleet north. Eventually, Edward landed at Ravenspur, the very place where King Henry's grandfather, Henry Bollingbroke, had returned to England to begin a journey that ended upon the throne. The omens were no doubt good.

York allowed Edward to enter on condition his army remained outside the city and the former king began to claim, as Bollingbroke had done, that he sought not the Crown but only the restoration of his Ducal lands and titles. Significantly, neither Montagu nor the restored Henry Percy sought to hinder or apprehend Edward. Though they did not overtly support him, neither did they block his progress. Beginning to move south, he gathered support and men as he entered more friendly territory in the Midlands.

Warwick was alerted to Edward's return and, leaving his brother George Neville in control of London, he took an army north and sent out a call to arms. Now, Margaret's hesitations and delays began to play into Edward's hands. Jasper Tudor, Edmund Beaufort, John Courtney, heir to the Dukedom of Devon and others were not keen to take up arms for Warwick. The turning of his coat left him swathed in suspicion, and their loyalty was to Henry and the more competent Margaret, not to Warwick. Lord Stanley also chose to ignore the summons, preferring to use the turmoil to pursue a feud with the Harrington family over possession of Hornby Castle. Oxford and Clarence did begin to mobilise and when he arrived at Coventry, Warwick still held the upper hand. Edward was blocked to the south by Warwick, the north by Montagu and on either flank by Oxford and Clarence.

Caught in a tightening noose, Edward acted decisively. He marched directly at Warwick, who promptly sealed himself within Coventry and awaited aid. Around this time, Clarence appears to have decided that his best hope now lay back with his brother and defected once more. Finding Coventry impenetrable, Edward could not lay a lengthy siege when other forces closed in about him. Edward decided to make a huge gamble. He rode for London, hoping to secure the city, the person of King Henry and a base from which to operate with authority. Now it was London caught in the jaws of a dilemma. Margaret was due to arrive any day. Edward was marching to the City with a large force of men and Warwick had sent word that under no circumstances was Edward to be allowed to enter. The earl was traditionally incredibly popular in London, but fear got the better of the City.

George Neville paraded King Henry through the streets in an attempt to firm up support, but the sight of the bewildered Henry being led by the hand by the Archbishop had the very opposite of the desired effect. Without any concept of the magnitude of the situation, Henry was like a spectator, not the main attraction, and support evaporated. Citing fear of casualties and an inability to resist an army, London opened its arms to Edward. Philippe de Commines offered other reasons for Edward's welcome, stating that merchants hoped for the repayment of substantial loans made to Edward whilst he was king and their wives hoped for a return to Edward's bed, persuading their husbands to support the return of the Yorkist king.

Edward installed his family in the Tower for safety, meeting his first born son and namesake for the first time, but he had no time for familial pleasantries. Warwick was bringing a huge army south. Gathering all of the men that he could, Edward marched north and the two forces met at the Battle of Barnet on Easter Sunday, 14th April 1471. Warwick had around 15,000 men led by Oxford, Montagu and Exeter whilst Edward commanded only about 10,000, leading the centre himself with Hastings on his left and his inexperienced young brother Richard, Duke of Gloucester getting his first taste of battle on the right flank.

The fighting was close and confused. In the darkness of the night the forces had drawn up close to each other and offset. Added to this, the dawn was foggy. Seizing the initiative, Edward ordered an all out attack. As the misaligned forces clashed there was confusion until Oxford's force overcame Hastings and moved to support their own middle. Mistaking Oxford's Stars with Rays badge for Edward's Sunne in Splendour emblem, the Lancastrian centre attacked their reinforcements and in the confusion treason and betrayal was screamed into the fog. In the debacle that followed, John Neville was slain. Seeing his brother felled, Warwick made for his horse to flee but was apprehended by Yorkist soldiers who dragged him to the ground and stabbed him in the neck. The Neville brothers' bodies where publically displayed in St Paul's Cathedral as proof of their final demise before being laid to rest in the family vault at Bisham Abbey. So ended the Maker of Kings.

Edward had little time to rest. Margaret had landed. Somerset was given charge of her army and now the Earl of Devon and Jasper Tudor mobilised. Edward mustered more men in London before setting out to meet the Lancastrian forces. The opposing armies manoeuvred along the Severn before they finally met at Tewkesbury. On 4th May 5,000 men lined up with King Edward, his commanders once more the loyal Hastings and Gloucester, who had proven himself no mean warrior at Barnet. The Lancastrian force of 7,000 was commanded by the Duke of Somerset and Earl of Devon. Crucially, Edward of Westminster, Prince of Wales was also upon the field. At 17, he was ambitious and perhaps expected his father to abdicate in his favour when all was resolved. With the two key protagonists of each side upon the battlefield, it would be settled that day.

The Yorkist force routed the Lancastrians and in the retreat, Edward of Westminster was killed. With him died any real hope for the future of Lancastrian rule. Somerset was captured and executed. The distraught Queen Margaret was taken prisoner and paraded through London as King Edward returned in triumph on 21st May. That night, King Henry VI died in the Tower of London. It was reported publically that he died of 'pure displeasure and melancholy' upon hearing the fate of his son and the failure of his cause. It seems far more likely though that Edward ordered him killed. Whilst he had an heir, it had suited Edward to keep the ineffectual Henry alive. His death then would have revitalised the Lancastrian cause in his much more promising son. With that son dead, Henry was now only a liability. Once Tewkesbury had been lost, Henry's fate had been sealed.

The Battle of Tewkesbury saw the extinction of the Lancastrian line. The Beaufort family, their distant cousins and potential heirs, were also wiped out in the male line. All that remained was the daughter of the 1st Duke, Lady Margaret Beaufort and her son, Henry Tudor, who was whisked to the continent by his uncle Jasper at the age of fourteen. Edward had won. York had won. Peace had arrived.

The Fifth Period

The Implosion Of The House Of York

With the light of Lancaster all but extinguished, Edward set about settling the House of York as the new ruling family. Over the next decade or so, he and Elizabeth extended their family to eventually total eight children who survived infancy, crucially including two sons. Edward had been born in sanctuary and the next child was another son, named Richard. In spite of his earlier betrayals, George was welcomed back into the fold and forgiven, though perhaps watched more closely. Richard married the recently widowed Anne Neville and the king's two brothers divided up the immense Warwick inheritance between them. Clarence took the Midlands and Marches whilst Richard acquired the lands and estates of the Neville heartland in Yorkshire.

As a mark of their dominance, the bodies of their father, Richard, Duke of York and brother Edmund who had both died at Wakefield in 1460 were moved from Pontefract to Fotheringhay in a lavish yet solemn procession that conferred upon the bodies the respect that they were now due. Richard settled in at Middleham Castle, where he had spent time as a child, and proved invaluable to Edward in settling the unruly north. Recognised for his good lordship,

Richard enforced peace at the Scottish borders and became popular and well loved.

By contrast, George never seemed to be able to reconcile himself to his brother's rule. When his wife Isabel died shortly after childbirth in 1476, perhaps of tuberculosis, he went into a rage, accusing one of her servants, Ankarette Twynyho of poisoning her. George had Ankarette executed with no due process and there was outrage, not least from Edward. By 1478, George had exhausted all of his brother's good will. As he began to resurrect the rumours of Edward's parentage, the king could endure his threat no longer. In 1478, Clarence was executed on Edward's orders. Reputedly allowed to decide the method of his own execution, George supposedly had himself drowned in a vat of the king's malmsey wine. As a member of the royal family, the execution took place in private and no sure record of it survives to confirm or refute this anecdote.

Crisis was to once again engulf the Crown in 1483, following a dozen years of settled peace. There is some evidence that in the early 1480's Edward was contemplating marrying his eldest daughter to the last, flickering candle of the Lancastrian line, Henry Tudor. Tudor would have been allowed to return from his exile and rejoin his mother, Margaret Beaufort, now married to Thomas, Lord Stanley. The significance for Edward would also have been obvious - with Lancaster's last hope reconciled, no threat to him or his son would remain. This work was, however, to remain incomplete.

On 9th April 1483, a few weeks short of his forty first birthday, King Edward IV died. A tall, athletic figure in his younger days, the years of peace had seen him indulge his appetite for food and women to excess. His court was considered a licentious centre of debauchery and his girth had grown along with his indulgence. After a short illness Edward died. He lingered long enough to alter his will, naming his loyal brother Richard as Lord Protector during the minority of his twelve year old son. Perhaps fearing the unpopularity of a Woodville controlled government and the reflection that it would cast upon his heir, Edward turned to the brother of royal blood who had served him without fault for almost fifteen years.

The events of 1483 have become clouded with the passing of time so that each event can have polar opposite meaning dependent upon the view of Richard taken. They are dealt with in more detail in A Glimpse of King Richard III. Richard, either genuinely or to cover his true intentions, began to fear a Woodville plot to exclude him from government. They intended to crown Edward V swiftly and declare him of age to rule, thus negating the need for Richard's Protectorate. Edward left Ludlow Castle with his household, led by the queen's brother Anthony, Earl Rivers. Richard arranged to meet them at Northampton to accompany his nephew, the new king, into London. The king's party went beyond

Northampton to the Woodville manor at Stoney Stratford, from where Earl Rivers rode back to meet Richard. Either sensing a plot or seizing his opportunity, Richard arrested Rivers, rode to Stoney Stratford and took control of the king, also arresting others of his household.

Edward V rode into London in triumph, accompanied by his uncle Richard and Henry Stafford, Duke of Buckingham upon whom Richard had called for aid. Edward was installed in the royal apartments in the Tower of London. Crucially, he was not imprisoned there as is often asserted. The Tower was a royal palace and was yet to acquire its more gruesome reputation. It would have been the natural place for Edward to prepare for his coronation.

Elizabeth Woodville had taken sanctuary within Westminster Abbey with her other children upon hearing of Richard's actions at Stoney Stratford, doubtless fearful of his intentions. Richard asked that her younger son, Richard, Duke of York be allowed to join his brother to provide him with comfort. After the exertion of some force, young Richard was sent to join Edward. Whilst all of this was happening, Council continued preparations for Edward's coronation. Coins began to be minted and proclamations made in his name. The establishment seemed pleased with Richard's bloodless removal of the upstart Woodvilles.

Council approved Richard as Protector, though only for a short period, with a further decision on an extension to be made later. They refused Richard's request to try Earl Rivers and the others arrested at Stoney Stratford for treason. Also, George Neville died without issue and this left Richard dangerously exposed. Edward IV had tied his brother's Neville inheritance to the survival of the line of George Neville, Duke of Bedford. This was perhaps a form of protection for the effectively disinherited George; as Warwick's nephew he had been the heir to his uncle's fortune. It may have also been an attempt to rein in Richard's own power. Whatever the reason, it backfired now as Richard's position became less stable. The Protector wrote to York asking for an armed force to be sent to protect him from plots and threats. This is perhaps made more suspicious by what was to follow.

At a meeting of the Council, Richard had Lord Hastings, Edward IV's closest friend and advisor arrested and executed for treason, claiming that there was a plot against him. This incident is another key moment in establishing what was happening. No trace of a plot remains for us to see, but that does not mean that it wasn't real. Hastings' ruthless execution, probably with no trial, is possibly the second darkest contributor to Richard's reputation. He was either both justified and decisive or he was a ruthless murderer.

Edward's coronation was due to take place on 22nd June 1483. Instead, on that date, a sermon was preached by Dr Ralph Shaa entitled 'Bastard Slips Shall

Not Take Deep Root'. This sermon, attended by Richard and Buckingham, made public a story that had been brought to Richard by Bishop Stillington, who claimed to be party to a pre-contract of marriage between Edward IV and Lady Eleanor Butler. The pre-contract allegedly took place before Edward's marriage to Elizabeth Woodville and although Lady Eleanor Butler was dead by 1483, she had been alive at the time of the wedding of Edward and Elizabeth. A pre-contract to marry was equivalent to a marriage. Under church and civil law, it was valid, making Edward's marriage to Elizabeth bigamous and its issue, including young Edward V, illegitimate and incapable of succeeding to the throne.

The sermon also dragged the issue of Edward IV's legitimacy back into the light. There had long been a rumour in France. King Louis XI was fond of promulgating it and both Warwick and Clarence had used against the king, perhaps the former making the latter aware of it. The rumour was that Edward was himself illegitimate, the son of an affair with an English archer named Bleybourne. Richard dropped this charge quickly, perhaps because his mother was in the City and he did not wish to upset her, or perhaps because he could not prove it. The allegations levelled at the legitimacy of Edward V were, though, proved to the satisfaction of Parliament. Richard was petitioned to take the throne as the senior legitimate claimant. Accepting the call, he was crowned King Richard III on 6th July 1483.

It has become almost impossible to determine the truth of these matters at such a distance. John Ashdown-Hill makes a strong case for the existence of the Butler pre-contract, which would legally have made Richard the legitimate king. The case was proven to Parliament, but it can be argued that Richard was in control of the political scene by that point and could have arranged Parliament's horrified acceptance of the news. As part of the campaign against his excesses, Edward IV's long term mistress Jane Shore, also the mistress of Lord Hastings and Thomas Grey, Elizabeth Woodville's son by her first marriage, was forced to do public penance for her misdemeanours by walking barefoot in just her petticoats through London's streets before a cross and a choir, the traditional punishment for a harlot. It was part of a propaganda campaign against Edward IV's rule. The reputation that had seen London wives aid his return to power in 1471 now undid his son.

The reputation of King Richard III has long been defined by the fate of his nephews, Edward V and Richard, Duke of York. Over the summer of 1483 they were seen less and less, moved to apartments deeper within the Tower of London before disappearing from public sight. Their story is dealt with in more detail in A Glimpse of The Princes in the Tower, but the uncertainty of their fate was to afflict King Richard. The embers of the Lancastrian cause glowed softly in exile. As Richard alienated those who had been loyal to his brother, the fading fire hungrily eyed fresh fuel.

At the end of the summer, a rebellion erupted. Named Buckingham's Rebellion, its initial aim was to free and restore Edward V, but amid rumour he and his brother were dead it quickly shifted to calling for Henry Tudor to return from exile and take the throne. Tudor left Brittany and Buckingham raised an army in Wales. A force from Kent attacked London too early, before the appointed date and alerted Richard to the plot. Raging storms favoured the king, flooding the River Severn to prevent Buckingham crossing and scattering Tudor's fleet. Eventually, Tudor limped back to Brittany and Buckingham was captured and executed.

Praised for the justice his only Parliament brought, Richard was nevertheless besieged by problems. To balance the disloyalty shown by those in the south he imported familiar, trusted men from the north. This in turn caused further resentment. Latent Lancastrian sympathy was swelled by Edwardian loyalists who would not accept Richard's rule. Richard made efforts to gain control of Tudor, but he escaped Brittany for France. There, disaffected Yorkists found a warm welcome and Lancastrians found hope. The Earl of Oxford escaped his long term prison in Calais, providing Tudor's faux court with the military expertise it had lacked. It soon became a question not of if an invasion would come, but when.

Bosworth

King Richard III's personal life began to unravel as his political grip on his kingdom slipped. On 9th April 1484, Richard and Anne's precious only child Edward of Middleham died aged 10. The couple were naturally distraught. Although the end of that year saw reconciliation with Elizabeth Woodville that brought her and her daughters out of sanctuary, 16th March 1485 marked further disaster. Anne Neville died, possibly of the same tuberculosis that killed her sister Isabel. Richard was a widowed, childless 32 year old king. All of that made him vulnerable. It was later rumoured that he had poisoned Anne in order to marry his own niece, Elizabeth of York. In fact, Richard, in need of stability, opened negotiations to marry himself and his niece into the Portuguese royal family. Time, though, was not on his side.

On 8th August Henry Tudor landed at Milford Haven in Wales. Richard had known he was coming but had believed he intended to land at the south coast. Tudor marched across Wales, gathering some support, though perhaps not as much as he may have hoped for. Richard called upon his nobles and the Duke of Norfolk, John Howard came with his son, as did Northumberland and Lord Stanley.

The two forces met at Bosworth Field on 22nd August 1485. Tudor had assembled around 5,000 men, mainly French mercenaries and Welshmen.

Richard had around 6,000 men with him and Norfolk, including those men of the north fiercely loyal to him, men like Richard Ratcliffe and Sir James Harrington. Henry Percy, Earl of Northumberland fielded about 3,000 men and Lord Stanley brought his own sizeable force, numbering around 4,000. The odds appeared firmly in the king's favour.

After an exchange of canon fire and arrow, the Duke of Norfolk engaged Tudor's army, led by the Earl of Oxford, one of the most experienced military men of the time. Oxford pressed hard and Norfolk himself was slain when Richard spotted Tudor and a small detachment moving across the back of the field toward Lord Stanley's position. Northumberland was ordered to engage but did not, for reasons that are not entirely clear. He may have been blocked by the terrain or he may have betrayed Richard.

Lord Stanley was an unknown quantity from the outset. He was Henry Tudor's step father and reputedly met with Tudor before the battle, pledging his support. He had also nominally taken the field for King Richard. His refusal to engage for either side effectively evened the numbers of each army and Tudor may well have been riding to encourage his step father to support him. With the battle not going as planned, Richard saw a chance to end the matter once and for all. With his household knights he charged Tudor's group. As Richard's men became overwhelmed, Stanley sent his brother Sir William and his men into the fray to finish off the king. Richard fell fighting, as even his critics were to concede, 'manfully in the thickest press of his enemies'.

Lord Stanley supposedly found Richard's crown and placed it upon Henry's head, thus beginning the reign of King Henry VII and the rule of the Tudor dynasty. The story of the Wars of the Roses, though, was not to stop at Bosworth with the death of the last Plantagenet king.

The Fight For The White Rose

Henry Tudor dated his reign from 21st August 1485, the day before Bosworth. It was an early sight of the propaganda tactics that were to define the Tudors. It allowed him to name all of those who took the field against him for King Richard as traitors. Henry had sworn to marry Elizabeth of York, daughter of Edward IV, to unite the Houses of York and Lancaster. He did not, however, finally marry Elizabeth until after his own coronation. Although he blamed the delay on the need for a papal dispensation for the wedding because of the couple's blood relationship, it is likely Henry was once more being shrewd. In order to marry Elizabeth and pacify her Yorkist supporters who had helped him to his throne, he had to re-legitimise her. This gave her better claim to the throne than he possessed, and Henry could not tolerate accusations that he ruled by virtue of his wife if he was to have any authority. He was also wary of becoming king by right of conquest, choosing instead to call upon his own scant Lancastrian roots. His rule would be a continuation of Lancastrian rule, correcting the evils of King Richard III. It was not an uprooting, it was a comfortable resettlement.

Uniting the White Rose of York with the Red Rose of Lancaster gave us the powerful iconography of the Tudor Rose that still surrounds us today. The Beaufort portcullis symbol of Henry's mother is to this day the emblem of Parliament. The Tudors imposed themselves upon England, embossing their identity into the country they now ruled, but the fight did not end at Bosworth. The White Rose would not be so easily consumed into the Tudor symbology.

In 1486, an attempt to rise against Henry was orchestrated by Francis, Lord Lovell and Sir Humphrey and Thomas Stafford who had survived Bosworth. The Stafford brothers held Worcester for a time but the uprising lacked a figurehead and was quickly quashed. Sir Humphrey was hung as a traitor, though Thomas was pardoned, and Francis Lovell escaped to Burgundy and the court of Margaret the Dowager Duchess of Burgundy. Sister to Edward IV and Richard III, Margaret was to prove a thorn in the side of the new Tudor Rose for many years.

With Burgundy's support, Francis Lovell landed with an army to place Edward, Earl of Warwick upon the throne. Edward was the son of George, Duke of Clarence. He was held in the Tower of London, yet Lovell brought with him a boy who was proclaimed to be the earl in Ireland. The king's army, led once more by Oxford, met the rebels at the Battle of East Stoke on 16th June 1487. Henry's army outnumbered the Yorkists 15,000 to 8,000 and crushed the invading force decisively. John de la Pole, Earl of Lincoln, previously King Richard's heir, had joined the rebellion but died at Stoke. Francis Lovell was seen fleeing the battlefield but then disappears from the historical record.

The boy that had accompanied the invading army was exposed as an imposter named Lambert Simnell, schooled to impersonate Warwick. It remains possible that he was in fact the true earl, though Henry paraded the boy in the Tower to prove that he was not. He would later do the same with Perkin Warbeck, a young man identified by Margaret of Burgundy as her nephew, Richard, Duke of York and recognised as legitimate by many of the crowned heads of Europe. It is a testament to the mystery surrounding the fate of the Princes in the Tower that none, including Henry, seemed too sure that he was not in fact Richard.

The de la Pole family, the brothers of John, were to prove a nuisance and threat to both Henry VII and his son Henry VIII. The last threat died with Richard de la Pole in 1525 at the Battle of Pavia. Henry VIII reportedly rejoiced at the news. As Henry VIII's health failed and his succession seemed insecure, there was further White Rose bloodletting. Henry VII had executed both Perkin Warbeck and Edward, Earl of Warwick in 1499, but Clarence also had a daughter. She had married a knight, Sir Richard Pole. Her third son Reginald had sided with Rome during the Reformation, much to the disgust of Henry VIII who had paid for his education. A supposed plot to resurrect the cause of the White Rose was exposed in 1538 and Margaret and two of her other sons were arrested. One son, Geoffrey, was pardoned but the other, Henry, was executed. On 27th May 1541, the 67 year old Margaret was dragged to the block and held down, struggling. The executioner took eleven strokes to kill her.

Reginald Pole became a Cardinal and plotted to reinstall Catholicism in England from the Continent. A marriage was suggested between him and Henry VIII's daughter Mary to effect the change and bring the White Rose back to power, but it did not happen. He did become Archbishop of Canterbury during Queen Mary's reign, dying in 1558. He was the final White Rose threat faced by the Tudors almost 75 years after they had come to the throne. The Wars of the Roses did not truly end at Bosworth and the Tudors always feared it growing too strong in their new garden. For all that they are imbedded into English history and culture, they were never quite as secure as they wished the world to believe.

Conclusion

The period of civil war called the Wars of the Roses is traditionally viewed as lasting from 1455 to 1485, from Richard, Duke of York's attempt to unseat King Henry VI until his own son, King Richard III was defeated at Bosworth. In reality, the roots of this conflict lay long before it erupted. As the large and ambitious royal family created by King Edward III began to feud and squabble, trouble moved ever closer. As unpopular as King Richard II was, his removal in favour of his cousin broke a line of male succession that stretched back 300 years to King Henry II. Unseating God's anointed King of England was previously unthinkable. Henry Bollingbroke made it an option, a choice in the face of poor kingship. He opened a door through which his own grandson was to be pushed, dragging a bickering nobility and a terrified country with him.

Ultimately, King Henry VI's weak rule, his strong willed wife Margaret of Anjou and the couple's preferment of the Beaufort Dukes of Somerset was to set the country on a course so reminiscent of the removal of King Richard II that Henry's own removal must have seemed not only feasible but desirable. Richard, Duke of York's handling of the matter was initially applauded. His Protectorate a time of even handed peace. Yet by the end of the 1450's he had lost control of the situation, but had travelled too far to stop. His son was to complete his work, yet not fully for over a decade more, hauling the country through more uncertainty and bloodletting.

King Richard III may have truly believed that his duty required him to take the throne or he may have perceived a situation so threatening to him that he had to act, but once more the removal of a king seemed an option rather than a sin. Unable to reconcile parts of the country to his rule, some of the most crucial and powerful parts, Richard lost his Crown to the unlikeliest of kings, Henry VII, who arrived with little hope yet played the game better than Richard had, recognising the need to attract the support of those who could win him the Crown. In him, latent Lancastrian hope and disaffected Yorkist hearts found a welcome home and he used this to unseat another king, the fourth removal of a monarch in under a hundred years. His success lay in his understanding and manipulation of the winds of politics.

Neither did the War of the Roses end conclusively at the Battle of Bosworth in 1485. The last pitched battle was to take place two years later at East Stoke and pretenders were to constantly harass Henry VII in the name of the White Rose. Even Henry VIII was so terrified of the faction that he at least believed plotted against him, whether it did in truth or not, that executions based solely upon Yorkist blood were still taking place in 1540's with Reginald Pole at least evading him until after that king's own death.

It is also worth considering the impact of small, local feuds. Many of these were settled under the guise of the war for the Crown. Many were to decide loyalties or push men of power from or toward one side or another, frequently dependent upon which side best served their own interests. Warwick is remembered as the Kingmaker, but he was only the most powerful of many seeking to improve their own lot or right wrongs, perceived or real.

The Wars of the Roses is a fascinating era that has contributed to the defining of England, not least because it placed the Crown finally upon the head of first of the Tudors who were to remake England in ways both positive and negative. The amount of subtle political manoeuvring and careful placement of alliances both within England and abroad by those hoping to influence or destabilise for their own ends is infinitely fascinating and seems to force people to take a side, even now.

This period of English history is supremely summed up by George R.R. Martin in his Song of Fire and Ice series of novels: "When you play the game of thrones, you win, or you die." For so many during this period, that was a fact of everyday life.

Further Reading

Bosworth: Birth of the Tudors, Chris Skidmore (W&N)

The History of England Volume 1: Foundation, Peter Ackroyd (Pan Books)

Lancaster & York: The Wars of the Roses, Alison Weir (Vintage)

Blood Sisters: The Women Behind the Wars of the Roses, Sarah Gristwood (Harper Press)

Printed in Great Britain
by Amazon

87249709R00061